Wonderfully Made

Debbie DiNardo

Illustrated by Andrew and Elisa DiNardo

Dedication

I dedicate this book to my husband, John, and our twins, Andrew and Elisa. Your love, creativity, and support not only made this book possible, you also made my dream come true! I love you more than all the stars in the sky!

About the Author

Debbie is a high school teacher of special needs students and has been writing poetry ever since she was a child, but she has never created a book out of any of her work until now. One day her young twins had an amazing idea of creating a book to help kids feel special, and she loved the opportunity to work together on such a soulful project. Her twins, Andrew and Elisa, created the illustrations to accompany her poem.

Just like each and every star in the sky,

Wonderfully made and unique, am I.

Just like each beautiful leaf that grows on a tree,

I am made special; there is only ONE me!

The TV shows us lots of toys and objects that we should buy,

Shiny new things that are fun — oh my!

I do not need those things; they just want to make money,

I am AWESOME...

just the way I AM,

SMART, KIND, and FUNNY!

We are ALL wonderfully made,

from the tops of our heads to the tips of our toes,

From our different types of hair, face shape,

eye colour and nose.

We may be different on the outside,

but inside, we are ALL the SAME,

We each have lungs, a heart, and a wonderfully

SMART brain!

When you wake up every single day,

Look in the mirror and say...

I LOVE YOU,

I really,

really

DO.

You are

AMAZING,

just by being YOU!

We are all works of art

each a masterpiece in the making,

If we believe in ourselves,

the future is ours for the taking!

We can be whatever we dream to be,

Our futures can be so exciting to see!

You can DO anything if you just believe,

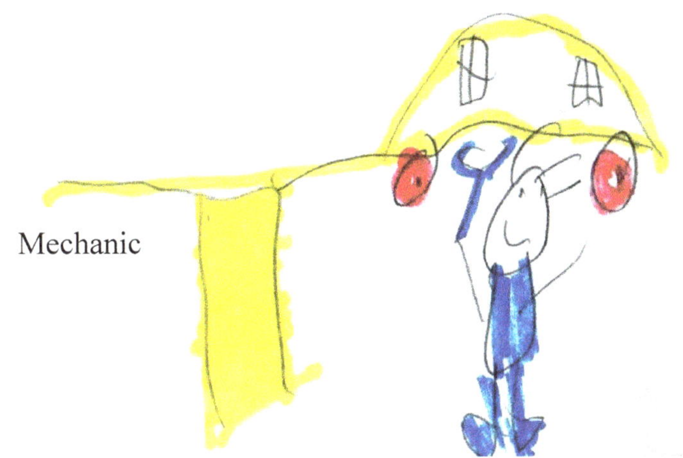

Mechanic

That all your dreams, you can achieve.

Teacher

Like every star lighting up the night,

You are meant to sparkle so bright.

Let your light shine — not ever fade,

Just keep on being you,

for YOU are Wonderfully Made!

WE
ARE
special